TIMELINES

1980s

by
Jane Duden and
Gail B. Stewart

CRESTWOOD HOUSE
New York

Collier Macmillan Canada
Toronto

Maxwell Macmillan International Publishing Group
New York   Oxford   Singapore   Sydney

Library of Congress Cataloging-in-Publication Data

Duden, Jane, date.

  1980s / by Jane Duden and Gail B. Stewart — 1st ed.

    p. cm. — (Timelines)

  Summary: Photographs and articles present the history, trivia, and fun of modern life between 1980 and 1989.

  ISBN 0-89686-599-1

  1. United States—History—1969– —Miscellanea—Juvenile literature. 2. History, Modern—1945– —Miscellanea—Juvenile literature. [1. History, Modern—1945– —Miscellanea.] I. Duden, Jane. II. Title. III. Series: Timelines (New York, N.Y.)

E855.S74   1991

909.82'8—dc20
                                      90-46827

                                                    CIP

                                                    AC

Photo Credits

Cover: Fotex: I. Rohrbein

All interior photos courtesy of AP—Wide World Photos

Special thanks to Marcia Lein

Copyright © 1991 Crestwood House, Macmillan Publishing Company

CRESTWOOD HOUSE

Macmillan Publishing Company
866 Third Avenue
New York, NY 10022

Collier Macmillan Canada, Inc.
1200 Eglinton Avenue East
Suite 200
Don Mills, Ontario M3C 3N1

Produced by Flying Fish Studio

Printed in the United States of America

First Edition

10 9 8 7 6 5 4 3 2 1

CONTENTS

Mikhail Gorbachev on the cover of Time

INTRODUCTION

The 1980s were a roller coaster of change. The best of times came right along with the worst of times. In the United States, prosperity marked the beginning of the decade. But a growing budget deficit, troubles on Wall Street, and increasing homelessness soon followed.

Ronald Reagan and Mikhail Gorbachev were the giants among world leaders. They broke up the Cold War ice jam and created a new chance for peace. The decade seemed to mark the beginning of the end for Communist police states. A new era of openness looked possible for the nineties. For his role in these great changes, Mikhail Gorbachev became *Time* magazine's Man of the Decade.

Satellites and fiber optics, TV and the fax wrapped us in a crazy quilt of information. The global population increased by over 800 million people, and problems grew just as fast. Hunger, terrorism, drugs, AIDS and pollution were worldwide troubles. Environmental disasters raised new concern for the condition of Planet Earth. While none of these issues was solved in the eighties, they hinted at the challenges that must be faced in the 1990s. The 20th century raced on!

SCANDAL!

In February 1980 it was revealed that FBI agents had been watching certain U.S. senators and representatives for two years. It was believed that some public officials were taking bribes in exchange for granting political favors. To prove those charges, FBI agents went undercover, pretending to be wealthy Arab businessmen. They offered senators and representatives thousands of dollars to use their power to help these "businessmen" in their ventures. The investigation had a code name: Abscam (a combination of "Abdul," an Arab name, and "scam").

Of course, the public officials had no way of knowing the whole thing was a setup. They did not know they were being filmed by secret cameras. A number of these films were later shown on television. The whole nation saw some of their elected officials accepting $50,000 bribes. When the Abscam investigation was complete, 19 officials—including seven members of Congress—were indicted on counts of conspiracy and accepting bribes.

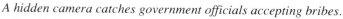

A hidden camera catches government officials accepting bribes.

The most expensive stamp

THE MOST EXPENSIVE 1¢ STAMP

In April the rarest stamp in the world was sold at an auction in New York City. The stamp was from British Guiana (now known as Guyana), a small nation in South America. It had been issued in 1856 for the price of 1¢. The stamp was sold in 1980 for $850,000.

FAST-MOVING BOOKS

In 1980 the public library in Billerica, Massachusetts, moved to a new location—about 1,000 feet away from the old library. There was a problem: Hiring workers to move all the books would be too expensive for the little town.

To save money, 300 people volunteered to make a human chain stretching from the old library to the new. Each book was passed from person to person until the job was done. Professional movers had estimated the job would take the better part of a week. The proud citizens of Billerica finished handing off the last book at the end of one day!

AMERICA'S 40TH PRESIDENT

Ex-actor Ronald Reagan, a Republican, beat Democrat Jimmy Carter in the November presidential election. Reagan promised in his campaign speeches to end the increasing unemployment in America. At 69 years of age, Reagan became the oldest elected president in U.S. history.

Smoke rises from the crater of Mount St. Helens.

VOLCANO ERUPTS IN THE NORTHWEST

No volcano on the mainland United States had erupted since 1917. But on May 18, 1980, all of that changed. Mount St. Helens, a usually quiet volcano in southwestern Washington, erupted. Fire and lava blasted more than 60,000 feet into the air. Ash from the volcano rained down on places more than 500 miles away.

The eruption of Mount St. Helens triggered other disasters too. Earthquakes, flash floods and mud slides caused billions of dollars' worth of damage. Some 35 bodies were eventually found in the debris. And 25 people were declared missing and presumed dead.

THE DEATH OF A LEGEND

On December 8, former Beatle John Lennon was shot to death. A mentally ill fan shot Lennon as he was returning to his New York apartment after a recording session. Police reported that the murderer had stalked Lennon for days and had even gotten his autograph.

As word spread of the killing, hundreds of fans held a candlelight vigil outside Lennon's apartment building. The murderer was later sentenced to life in prison.

8

Mourning fans hold a vigil outside John Lennon's apartment building.

9

ATTACK OF THE MEDFLY

Early in 1981 California farmers met a frightening enemy. Called the Mediterranean fruit fly, or medfly for short, this tiny insect can destroy acres of fruits and vegetables. By the time the medflies were discovered, a large farming area in California was already contaminated.

Officials quarantined the area, making sure that no fruits or vegetables could be removed. People were stopped and searched to make sure they weren't carrying food with medflies on it. The area was sprayed to control the insects, but they remain a threat to this day!

AN EMOTIONAL HOMECOMING

On January 20, 52 American hostages held by Iranian terrorists were released. Their freedom came 444 days after they were seized during the takeover of the American embassy in Iran by the terrorists.

One of the American hostages cheers after being freed.

Bands, applause and homecoming parades greeted the hostages in New York City and Washington, D.C. Yellow ribbons were everywhere. For many months these had been the symbols of hope that the hostages would come home.

THE YEAR OF THE ASSASSIN

Many leaders were targets of assassins in 1981. President Anwar Sadat of Egypt was killed by political opponents at a military parade. On March 30, President Reagan was shot in the chest as he walked to his limousine after giving a speech in Washington, D.C. Doctors removed the bullet, and Reagan recovered quickly. His attacker, John Hinckley, Jr., was found not guilty by reason of insanity.

Less than two months later, Pope John Paul II was shot. The pope was riding in an open car through the streets of Rome. An escaped criminal from Turkey shot him twice in the abdomen. The pope recovered. His attacker was sentenced to life in prison.

FRUSTRATION!

In 1981 Hungarian designer Erno Rubik invented a difficult new puzzle. It was a large cube made up of 26 smaller colorful cubes that rotated. The object was to unscramble the small cubes until each side of the large cube was the same color. The puzzles, which are called Rubik's Cubes, caught on in the United States in a big way. By July 1981 over 10 million had been sold!

A young fan shows his disappointment during the baseball strike.

STRIKE—THE PLAYERS WALK!

In June and July, major league baseball is usually in full swing. However, in June 1981 all major league ballplayers went on strike. No games were played until the strike was settled on August 1.

12

AIDS FIRST IDENTIFIED

It was in 1981 that the deadly disease AIDS was first identified. Medical researchers learned that the virus that causes AIDS attacks a person's immune system. Not everyone who has the virus necessarily develops AIDS. But those who do cannot fight off disease or even minor infections. A person can get AIDS by having sexual contact with someone who has the virus or by sharing a needle with an infected person.

At first AIDS seemed to strike mostly gay men. But soon other people, including drug users and newborn babies of women with AIDS, were diagnosed with the disease. By the end of the decade, more than 1 million Americans were believed to be infected with the AIDS virus. Over 110,000 AIDS cases and more than 65,000 AIDS-related deaths had been reported in the United States.

IF AT FIRST YOU DON'T SUCCEED . . .

For 11 years, author John Kennedy Toole tried to find a publisher for his comic novel *A Confederacy of Dunces*. No one was interested. Finally, depressed and frustrated, Toole killed himself.

His mother did not give up, however. She tried to sell the story for 11 more years after her son's death. Her efforts paid off—with amazing results. The novel no one was interested in was finally published. And in 1981 *A Confederacy of Dunces* won the Pulitzer Prize, the highest honor for an American novel!

TREASURE FOUND!

Author Kit Williams wanted to make sure that the sales of his mystery novel for children would be brisk, so he included clues pointing to a real-life treasure in his book *Masquerade*. Whoever could find the hiding place could keep the treasure.

In 1982 a man who had read the book found a strangely shaped stone in the English countryside. It seemed to fit the description given in Williams's clues, so he began digging. Five days later he uncovered a beautiful golden medal!

CAN'T ANYBODY TAKE A JOKE?

For many years people in the American Northwest have been telling stories about a legendary creature called Bigfoot. Many say they have seen giant footprints. A few claim to have actually met the creature face-to-face.

In May 1982, an 86-year-old former forest ranger named Rant Mullens admitted that he had been making some of those footprints himself! Mullens said he made a set of big wooden feet and stomped around the forest wearing them. He enjoyed hearing campers and hikers talking excitedly about having seen "Bigfoot's prints." Even some of his friends got into the act, said Mullens. They borrowed the wooden feet and made footprints in other areas of Washington and Oregon.

GOOD DOG, DOOLEY

A California man was severely injured when his car rolled down a steep embankment in a remote area. His dog, Dooley, who had been riding with him, was unharmed and somehow climbed up the embankment. Dooley found his way home after two days and led family members to his master just in time!

14

NO NUKES

In June 800,000 people gathered in the streets of New York City. They were protesting the stockpiling of nuclear weapons. Many carried signs that read NUCLEAR WAR MEANS DEAD FOREVER. There were speeches and songs. It was the largest antinuclear arms rally ever held in the United States.

THE TYLENOL SCARE

In 1982 seven people in the Chicago area and one Californian died because they used Tylenol that had been tampered with. Someone had put the deadly poison cyanide into some capsules of the popular pain reliever.

Tylenol was quickly removed from the shelves of supermarkets and drugstores. Five weeks later the makers of Tylenol reintroduced the product, complete with tamper-proof packaging.

Tylenol is removed from shelves after tainted capsules were found.

A NEW MEMORIAL

The Vietnam War had been a source of conflict in the United States for a long time. Many Americans had been opposed to it. And many soldiers who had served in Vietnam found themselves scorned and ridiculed. In November an effort was made to honor those who had died in Vietnam and to heal the wounds that divided the country.

In Washington, D.C., a new monument was dedicated. Made of gleaming black granite, it listed the names of 50,000 American soldiers who had died or were missing in the Vietnam War.

People search the walls of the Vietnam War Memorial for the names of friends and relatives.

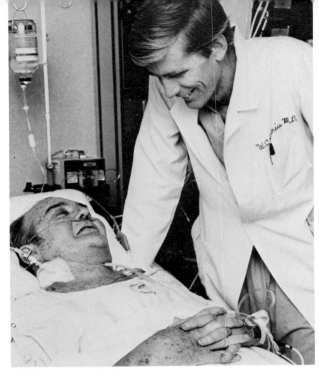

Barney Clark after receiving an artificial heart

A NEW HEART

Barney Clark, 61, was close to death in 1982. His heart was badly damaged and could not be repaired. In December doctors gave him a special new mechanical heart, called a Jarvik-7. Barney Clark was the first person ever to receive an artificial heart!

The Jarvik-7 had been tested on animals but not on people. No one knew for sure how a person's body would react to the mechanical heart. Doctors watched Clark closely for infection or poor blood circulation. Two weeks after receiving the mechanical heart, Barney Clark was able to get out of bed and walk for a few minutes. He hadn't been able to do that for some time.

Barney Clark would live for only 112 days after the operation. But he led the way for more successful mechanical-heart implants for others.

The cast of M*A*S*H

FAREWELL, HAWKEYE, HOT LIPS AND RADAR

After 10$^{1}/_{2}$ years, the hit TV series *M*A*S*H* ended on February 28. The comedy series about an American medical unit in the Korean War had won honors as one of the best shows ever on television. It was estimated that 125 million loyal viewers tuned in to watch the final episode.

A MERRY CHRISTMAS!

In 1983 a contest was held to design the 1984 Christmas stamp. This time the contest was open to children. Over half a million entries were judged. The winner was an eight-year-old boy from New York named Danny La Boccetta. His crayon drawing of a jolly Santa Claus was issued for the 1984 Christmas season.

CAN TREES TALK?

Two scientists from the University of Washington presented an interesting idea in 1983. They had done experiments to see if trees could communicate with one another. As it turned out, the scientists decided that trees may indeed "talk"!

The scientists put swarms of hungry leaf-eating caterpillars on one tree. Normally, when trees sense such caterpillars, they quickly create a bitter-tasting chemical on their leaves to keep the caterpillars from eating them. The scientists found that the trees near the one with the caterpillars also created the bitter chemicals! How did they know the caterpillars were nearby? The scientists decided that somehow—they didn't know quite how—the trees were letting one another know of the danger.

1983 FRAUD!

In April a West German magazine announced that it had uncovered the personal journal of Adolf Hitler's last years. The journal was very long—60 volumes—and handwritten. By publishing parts of the journal from week to week, the magazine would be sure to boost its circulation.

However, many scholars thought that the journal was a fake.

It was well known that Hitler did not like to write by hand. He preferred dictating letters and memos. After painstaking study and analysis, the journal was declared to be a forgery—although a good one. Soon after, a reporter for the magazine admitted that the whole thing had been a hoax.

WALESA WINS PEACE PRIZE

Polish union leader Lech Walesa won the Nobel Peace Prize in 1983. He was honored for helping to unify the working people of Poland in their efforts to better their lives. Walesa was not liked by Poland's Communist government, however. Fearing that he would not be allowed to return to Poland, Walesa did not travel to Oslo, Norway, to receive his award. His wife, Danuta, accepted the prize in his absence.

Lech Walesa, recipient of the Nobel Peace Prize in 1983

20

Rescue workers remove the injured following the terrorist attack against U.S. Marines in Lebanon.

TERRORISM IN LEBANON

In 1983 the United States had troops stationed in Beirut, Lebanon, to help keep peace between warring Moslems and Christians. On October 23, a U.S. Marine complex became the target of a terrorist attack. A terrorist drove toward the marine complex in a large truck wired with 25,000 pounds of explosives. As the truck hit the building, it became a bomb, killing 241 marines.

FIGHTING ACID RAIN

Governor Mario Cuomo of New York signed a new law in 1984. His state became the first to require factories to lower the amounts of sulfur dioxide they pump into the air. Sulfur dioxide mingles with moisture in clouds to form acid rain. By 1983 there was a great deal of evidence that acid rain was killing trees, lakes and wildlife. More states followed New York's example in the next few years.

Ray Kroc, founder of McDonald's

McDONALD'S FOUNDER DIES

In January, 81-year-old businessman Ray Kroc died. He was the founder of McDonald's, the most successful fast-food chain in the world. His goal was to serve simple food at an affordable price.

The first McDonald's opened in 1955 in Chicago. By the time of Kroc's death, the number of restaurants had grown to over 7,500—in 32 countries around the world!

THE BOY IN THE BUBBLE

On February 22 a very famous little boy died. His name was David, but he was better known as "the boy in the bubble." David was born with a malfunctioning immune system. His body was unable to fight off even the most minor infections.

As a tiny baby, David was placed in a sterile bubble where doctors could keep track of everything he touched, ate and breathed. If any germs touched David, his life would be in danger.

When David was 12, doctors tried to cure him by placing some of his sister's healthy bone marrow in his body. It was hoped that this new bone marrow could spark his immune system. For several days it seemed that David's problems might be over. He was able, for the first time, to live in a regular hospital room, outside of his bubble. But about two weeks later, David died.

David inside the plastic bubble that kept him alive

RATING MOVIES

It was in 1984 that a new movie-rating category was created: PG-13. Movies up to this time were rated "G" for "General Audiences" or "R" for "Restricted—no one under 17 admitted."

However, more and more movies were falling into the gap between "G" and "R." One such movie was *Indiana Jones and the Temple of Doom*, produced by Steven Spielberg. Spielberg himself wanted the new rating. He knew kids would want to see his new Indiana Jones movie, but he admitted that part of it was too gory and scary for many young people. The PG-13 rating would alert parents that some portions of otherwise "G" movies could be violent and frightening.

Harrison Ford as Indiana Jones

BABY FAE

Controversy broke out in 1984 when a 15-day-old baby named Fae received a heart transplant. Doctors at Loma Linda University Medical Center in California knew that the baby had a defective heart. The chances of receiving a suitable human heart for transplant were very slim, so doctors inserted a baboon's heart into Fae.

Animal-rights groups were angry about the killing of a baboon. Some religious groups felt that it was wrong to replace human organs with animal ones. Many in the medical community were angry with the Loma Linda doctors for testing such a farfetched idea on a human baby. Baby Fae died less than three weeks after her transplant.

THOUSANDS POISONED WITH DEADLY GAS

On December 3, a Union Carbide plant in Bhopal, India, sprang a leak in one of its underground storage tanks. A deadly gas called methyl isocyanate escaped, filling the air with poisonous fumes. Because the leak occurred in the middle of the night, many people were sleeping and could not escape. However, tens of thousands did flee, blinded by the stinging gas. Over 2,000 people died from inhaling the fumes, and more than 100,000 were injured. Many of these were small children whose sensitive eyes were burned by the gas. The area was littered with the bodies of insects, dogs, cats and thousands of birds.

Union Carbide, an American company, was criticized around the world for having a plant in such a densely populated area. Said one observer, "If a plant like this were located in a wealthy area of New York or Los Angeles, there would have been all kinds of safeguards. But because the location was a poor part of India, no one seemed to care."

Ronald Reagan is sworn in as the 40th president of the United States.

DOUBLE TAKE FOR REAGAN

Thanks to cold weather and play-offs for Super Bowl XIX, President Ronald Reagan was sworn into office twice. He took the oath of office for his second term on January 20. The oath was televised, but more Americans were tuned in to the 49ers and the Dolphins than the inauguration. Then the inauguration parade was canceled due to freezing weather. So President Reagan repeated the oath for TV viewers on January 21.

BETTER DAYS FOR SOVIETS

Mikhail Gorbachev became the new leader of the Soviet Union on March 11. Gorbachev promised to cut back on military spending. He would make it easier, he said, for Soviets to buy basics, like food and clothing. He would improve the Soviet economy. Gorbachev called his plans for improvement *perestroika*. That's the Russian word for restructuring. Before Gorbachev, people didn't dare complain about the government. Threats of jail or a labor camp kept them quiet. But Gorbachev changed that with his policy of *glasnost*, the Russian word for openness. Only time would tell if the new Soviet leader would be able to deliver a better quality of life to his people.

The new look of Classic Coke

STILL THE REAL THING?

For 99 years "Coke was it," but things changed in April. Coke's maker said a new formula would be in stores the next month. Pepsi quickly held a press conference, inviting reporters to taste "the *real* real thing." Would "things go better" with the new Coke? They did not. After only ten weeks on the market, New Coke fell flat. The old formula came back in July as Coca-Cola Classic. Just two months after its 100th birthday, Classic Coke was a hit and New Coke had fizzled out.

HOLE IN THE SKY

British scientists in Antarctica made a shocking announcement in May. In the atmosphere over the South Pole, a hole the size of the United States had opened up in the ozone layer.

Ozone is a natural gas in the earth's upper atmosphere. It is earth's only protection from the sun's harmful ultraviolet (UV) rays. The ozone hole was caused by the release of man-made chemicals called CFCs, used in foam packaging, coolants and other products. Less ozone means more UV. The effects of increased UV are serious. UV can be harmful to plants, animals and people. Even a small loss of the ozone shield can hurt crops and trees. It can upset ecosystems and increase cases of skin cancer in humans.

The ozone layer is thinning at other areas around the globe. To avoid threats to humans, wildlife and the environment, countries of the world began joining forces. They realized it would take all of us working together to protect the ozone layer.

BIGGER . . . STRONGER . . . FASTER

He was a skinny kid from Georgia who couldn't beat his sister in a race. So Herschel Walker took the advice of his high school track coach: "Do push-ups and sit-ups, and run sprints."

One year later Herschel had done more than 100,000 push-ups and more than 100,000 sit-ups. He had sprinted nearly 500,000 miles. After training for three more years, Herschel finally beat his sister in a race!

Herschel Walker's determination made him a star on the football field. In 1982 he won football's Heisman trophy. Then in 1985 he did something that no other pro running back had ever done. He rushed for 2,411 yards in one season. Herschel says, "People can't believe how little and slow I was. But I remember." Now he tells kids that if they want to become bigger, stronger, faster...do lots of push-ups, sit-ups and pull-ups!

Herschel Walker holding the Heisman trophy

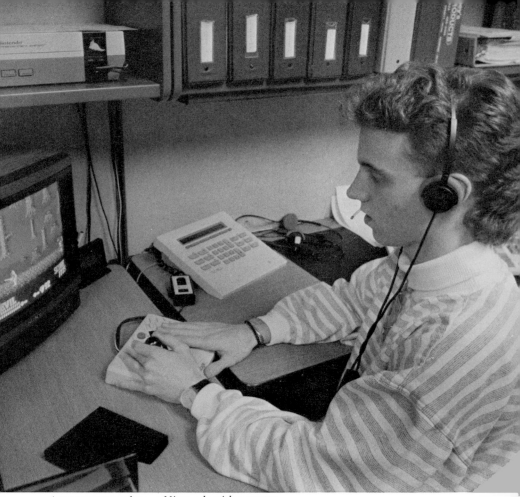

A young man plays a Nintendo video game.

BLEEP, BONK, ZOINK

Nintendo launched its home entertainment system in 1985. Home video games were so much fun that many kids quit saving quarters for video arcades. Mild-mannered eighth-graders rushed home from school to the video switches. They became cosmic warriors and space invaders. Some boxed with Mike Tyson. Others became knights battling dragons.

The crew of the space shuttle Challenger

THE *CHALLENGER* EXPLODES

The nation's 25th shuttle mission had been delayed for three days by bad weather. On January 28, 1986, all systems were GO. The space shuttle *Challenger* looked good at liftoff. But disaster struck 73 seconds later. The *Challenger* exploded in a ball of fire as millions of television viewers watched in horror. Cheers for *Challenger* faded into stunned silence. The shuttle broke apart. Thousands of pieces fell into the deep ocean waters off the coast of Florida. All seven crew members died, including the first teacher in space, Christa McAuliffe. Her students were among the millions of Americans watching on TV. The *Challenger* explosion was the worst accident in the history of the U.S. space program.

The *Challenger* tragedy brought the space program to a standstill. The nation mourned the seven *Challenger* heroes. And President Reagan pledged to honor them by not giving up on space exploration.

NUCLEAR POWER DISASTER

The world's worst nuclear accident occurred on April 26. It happened at Chernobyl, a nuclear power plant in the Soviet Union. A reactor exploded twice, causing huge amounts of radiation to escape into the atmosphere. At least 24 Soviets died from the effects of radiation poisoning. When radioactive particles are inhaled, swallowed or absorbed into the body, they may damage or destroy cells. When cells of vital organs are badly damaged, a person dies.

Fruits, vegetables and other fresh foods from Eastern Europe were banned when they showed high levels of radiation after the accident. In Poland children who were exposed when the radioactive cloud from Chernobyl passed over their country were given pills to cut down the effects of radiation. Scientists say that the fallout of radiation will affect the health of tens of thousands of Soviet citizens. Thousands of people will die over the next several decades due to medical problems caused by escaped radiation.

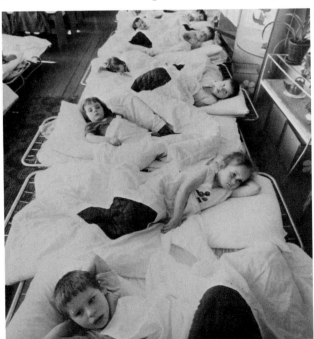

Children suffering from radiation sickness four years after the Chernobyl explosion

31

OLD STUFF IS NEW AGAIN

What were kids wearing when school doors opened in fall 1986? The "freshest" fashions were miniskirts, tie-dyed shirts, and bleached jeans. But how fresh were those styles? Not very—they were all popular in the 1960s! If you wonder where today's trends come from, check out your parents' closets. You might find clothes just like the ones you're wearing!

SUPER-LIGHT FLIGHT

Could you stand to live with a friend for nine days in a space the size of a telephone booth? Pilots Dick Rutan and Jeana Yeager made history doing just that. They shared the cockpit of a sleek plane called the *Voyager*. On December 23 they completed the first flight around the world without stopping or refueling. Some called the super-light *Voyager* a flying gas tank. It carried five times its weight in fuel. The *Voyager* was made of lightweight plastic and paper. The material weighed less than aluminum but was seven times stronger. The two-person crew set a record for endurance too. They were bruised and tossed by violent storms. They got little sleep. But they circled the globe in nine days, three minutes and 44 seconds without refueling. That's a record!

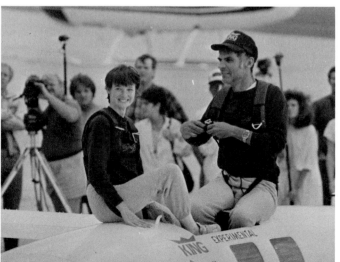

Dick Rutan and Jeana Yeager on top of the Voyager

Rear Admiral John Poindexter during the Iran-Contra trials

IRAN-CONTRA AFFAIR EXPLODES

It was the worst political scandal since Watergate. During November 1986, reports leaked out that the Reagan administration had secretly sold arms to Iran. Some of the profits were used to aid rebels fighting to overthrow the Communist government in Nicaragua. It had been the administration's policy never to sell arms to Iran and never to trade arms for the release of American hostages. Further, aiding rebels in Nicaragua was against the law in the United States. Congress had banned such activity. In the months ahead, the American public would hear a lot more about the Iran-Contra scandal as a congressional committee tried to uncover the whole truth.

GETTING CROWDED?

The population of the world topped 5 billion in 1986. A million people were added to the world every four or five days. In the last century the world population has more than tripled. By 1999 the world population is expected to reach 6 billion. The 7 billion mark will probably come in 2010, and 8 billion in 2025.

Where will all these people be? By the year 2000, Mexico City, with 27.9 million, will have more people than Tokyo. Three-fourths of the world's population will live in developing countries.

33

NO PLACE TO STASH TRASH

A barge called the *Mobro* left Islip, New York, in the spring of 1987. It was looking for a dumping ground for the 3,100 tons of garbage it carried. It sailed to North Carolina, Louisiana, Mexico and elsewhere. Every place the *Mobro* stopped, the answer was the same: Keep moving. No one wanted the smelly, fly-infested cargo. After 6,000 miles and 60 days, the *Mobro* went to New York Harbor, its rotting load still aboard. Brooklyn, New York, eventually burned the garbage in an incinerator. It turned into 400 tons of ash. The remains made a final trip home. Back in Islip, the ashes were dumped in the local landfill.

The *Mobro* was a reminder of a growing worldwide challenge. Where *do* we stash our growing mountains of trash? Many places are running out of space to put garbage. People began talking about the new three Rs: Reduce, Reuse, Recycle.

The Mobro *with its cargo of trash*

The AIDS memorial quilt

THE WORLD'S LARGEST QUILT

Its patchwork pattern spread for 1.73 acres on the lawn of the Capitol in Washington, D.C. Altogether, 1,920 squares were sewn together to create the world's largest quilt. Each panel showed the name of someone with AIDS who had died. Some squares were as plain as gravestones. Others had colorful designs and details about the person's life. The quilt was bigger than two football fields. Over 200,000 people gathered on October 11 to see the quilt and draw the nation's attention to AIDS.

A TOUCH OF MAGIC

He is known to the world as "Magic." Playing in guard position for the Los Angeles Lakers, Earvin "Magic" Johnson towers over most folks with his height of six feet, nine inches. In the 1987–88 season, he led the Lakers to the NBA's first back-to-back titles since 1969. He is also the all-time NBA play-off leader in assists and steals. What advice does Magic give young people? "Set your goals high, practice hard, and remember you are part of a team."

OLLIEMANIA

It was July 1987, and the Iran-Contra congressional hearings were under way. Millions of Americans watched them on television. It was indeed the stuff of drama.

Who were the key players? Marine Lieutenant Colonel Oliver North, who managed the Iran-Contra deal; his beautiful and loyal secretary, Fawn Hall, who shredded and altered memos to protect her boss; Robert McFarlane, former White House national security adviser, who attempted suicide after the scandal broke; and Rear Admiral John M. Poindexter, who claimed to be responsible for the decision to send arms-sale profits to Nicaragua. Key witness William J. Casey, former CIA director, died from a brain tumor just before testifying. His death meant that the whole truth would probably never be revealed.

"Olliemania" swept the country as Colonel North told his side of the story. He was viewed by some as loyal to America, by others as ignoring democratic processes. He drew more TV viewers than the soap operas and game shows!

SPARE THE AIR

By mid-1987, 39 states had approved laws restricting smoking. Some places limited smoking in government buildings. Others limited smoking in businesses and public areas such as restaurants.

CRASH!

Was history repeating itself? The stock market had boomed throughout the eighties, just as it had in the prosperous Roaring Twenties. But Wall Street had its worst day ever on October 19, 1987. On "Black Monday" the stock market fell 508 points. That was almost double the decline of the Wall Street crash in 1929 that ushered in the Great Depression.

Americans—and the world—feared it was the beginning of another Great Depression. But the panic eased somewhat as the stock market rose again in the following weeks. Gone, however, was the feeling of prosperity that marked the early eighties.

FILL 'ER UP WITH SUN POWER

Twenty-five solar-powered cars left Darwin, Australia, on November 1, 1987. They were headed across the hot desert between Darwin and Adelaide. Each was set on winning the first World's Solar Challenge Continental Race. But the race was never close. Sunraycer, the American entry, sped to the lead and won. Sponsored by General Motors, Sunraycer averaged 43.5 miles per hour. It reached top speeds of more than 70 miles per hour. Sunraycer traveled nearly 2,000 miles without using a drop of gasoline. The energy that powered the car came from the sun. About 7,200 solar cells covered the 20-foot-long car. The solar cells contained a special light-sensitive material. This material changed the sun's energy into electrical energy to run the car.

SUPERCONDUCTORS

Picture floating trains that travel at 300 miles per hour. Imagine tiny, super-fast computers and gasoline-free electric cars that need recharging only once a month. What will make all this possible? Superconductors—and they're here! In 1987 scientists announced the discovery of a superconductor compound that allows electricity to go through it super easily. No energy is lost, and the material stays cool. This exciting development in science will change our lives.

YOUR HIGH TOPS OR YOUR LIFE

In January, Eric Allen lost his life over a pair of tennis shoes. He was stabbed with a butcher knife by a 14-year-old star athlete in Houston, Texas. The two had argued over a pair of sneakers.

Such killings weren't new. Sneakers and team jackets were so hot that kids were being mugged and killed for them. The killers—often drug dealers and gang members—were not just after the clothes. They were after the status that comes from names like Nike, Reebok, Adidas and Fila.

Big-name sports heroes like Bo Jackson and Michael Jordan helped to advertise this athletic gear. Michael Jordan was sad and angry about the killings: "I'd rather eliminate the product [the shoes] than know drug dealers are providing the funds that pay me."

RARE BIRD!

Would the big blue-green egg at the San Diego Wild Animal Park hatch? From the day the egg was laid, it was watched over. Keepers tended it around the clock. Why all the fuss about one egg? If hatched, this egg would help to save a species from extinction. It was the first egg to be laid by a California condor in captivity.

There were once hundreds of California condors. With wingspans of up to ten feet, they are the largest birds in North America. Today California condors no longer live in the wilderness. The last wild condor was captured in April 1987. At that time only 27 California condors were left in the world. All were in captivity at the San Diego Wild Animal Park and the Los Angeles Zoo.

On April 29, 1988, the egg did hatch. Out came Molloko, the

world's 28th California condor—scruffy, bald, exhausted. Wildlife experts believe they can raise more chicks like Molloko. They hope someday to return condors to their true home in the wild.

HOW HIGH CAN HE FLY?

He's bad when he drives. He's even more dangerous when he flies. Michael Jordan is a basketball whirligig. He swoops downcourt for the Chicago Bulls with dizzying speed. He vaults into the air with skyscraper leaps to dunk a shot, then lands on his feet like a cat. In both 1987 and 1988 Jordan was the NBA Scoring Leader. He averaged the most points of any player in the league. "You have to expect things of yourself before you can do them," says Michael.

Michael Jordan

WHAT'S WRONG WITH OUR WEATHER?

During the summer of 1988, much of the United States roasted in a heat wave. Lawns turned crisp. Crops shriveled and failed. Cattle and wild animals died. Barges and ships ran aground in rivers with sinking water levels. Forest fires raged in Yellowstone National Park and other places. Dozens of people died from the heat. A drought was caused by a high-pressure air system that stalled over the central United States. It was one of the century's worst droughts.

Many scientists think that droughts will become more common in the future. They believe the earth is becoming a warmer place to live. Earth's average temperature has been rising for most of this century. The heating may be due to what scientists call the greenhouse effect, which is a theory that describes the way our atmosphere is trapping heat. Earth's atmosphere is heating up mostly because of man-made pollution.

In 1988 people everywhere became more concerned about the planet. They tried harder to save energy. They planted trees. They recycled more products. And more people joined the environmental movement, making it one of the greatest issues of our time.

A dried-up reservoir in Minnesota during the drought of '88

FloJo runs for the gold.

FASTEST WOMAN IN THE WORLD

During the 1988 Summer Olympics in Seoul, Korea, Florence Griffith Joyner set a new world record of 10:49 seconds in the 100-meter trial run. Most experts believe that this record will not be challenged for ten years. What makes FloJo run? She made a sign stating her goal to break a world record in the 100-meter run. She looked at it every day. Some mornings she just didn't want to get up. But she'd look at the sign and say, "If you want to be a gold medalist, you're going to have to get up out of bed right now and go on that run!" FloJo also used mental practice. She imagined reaching her goal. Her discipline paid off. The TV world was delighted to watch her win three gold medals.

Barbara Bush with Millie and the White House puppies

A FULL HOUSE

In January, George Bush was sworn in as the 41st president of the United States. George and Barbara Bush moved into the White House with their English springer spaniel, Millie. Millie went to the Oval Office every morning at seven to play and visit. But then she had puppies—five females and one male. Nancy Reagan's former beauty salon was the maternity ward. Millie's box was decorated with the presidential seal. What about Millie's pups? The Bush children and grandchildren got first pick.

FLIPPED OUT

Neil Smith, age 11, flipped the same pancake 270 times in three minutes. In February, Neil won the Pancake Flip-Off in Liberal, Kansas. It was the third year in a row that Neil had flipped without a slip!

ALASKA'S BIG SPILL

On March 24, 1989, something tragic happened in Alaska's Prince William Sound. An oil tanker called the *Exxon Valdez* veered into water that was too shallow. The ship's metal bottom scraped against the ocean floor and ripped open. More than one million barrels of thick, dark oil poured into the clean, cold water. It was the largest oil spill in U.S. history.

The wilderness near the Alaskan spill was one of the least polluted areas in the world. Volunteers laid long lines of floats to keep the oil from spreading. But only six days later, the oil slick covered 50 square miles—an area twice the size of San Francisco. The oil spill eventually fouled 1,000 miles of Alaskan shoreline. It wrecked the area's fishing industry. It killed thousands of seabirds and aquatic mammals.

The Exxon Valdez *(right) surrounded by spilled oil*

SAME DINOSAUR, DIFFERENT NAME

The U.S. Postal Service sent out more than 4 million sets of dinosaur stamps this year. Sets included a tyrannosaurus, stegosaurus, pteranodon and the one with the short legs, fat body and super-long neck. Did you say brontosaurus? That's what the postal service labeled it. But in 1974, scientists changed the dinosaur's name from brontosaurus to apatosaurus. The scientist who found the fossil bones in 1874 thought they were from an unknown dinosaur. He named the dino brontosaurus. Scientists later proved the fossils matched those of apatosaurus, a dino that had already been named.

It turns out that officials at the postal service knew the name on the stamp was wrong before it was printed. Why didn't they correct it? They felt most people did not know that brontosaurus should be called apatosaurus. The name might be a mistake, but the price stayed the same. The stamp still cost a quarter and a lick.

GREETINGS FROM SPACE

Voyager 2 passed close to the planet Neptune around midnight, August 24, 1989. It had been traveling through space since August 20, 1977. *Voyager 2* had already photographed Jupiter, Saturn and Uranus. Now it had finally reached far-off Neptune. But *Voyager 2*'s mission was not yet complete. It would continue its journey beyond the solar system, measuring activity between the stars.

If, by any chance, distant alien citizens were to discover *Voyager 2*, they would have a surprise. A gold-plated disc is attached to the side of the craft. The disc is a record with earth sounds. The aliens would hear singing whales, a cooing baby and greetings from earth in 60 languages. So. . . *Guten Tag! Bonjour! Hola!* . . . to any friends in outer space!

COWABUNGA DUDES!

Turtles who knew Ninja-jitsu began to show their Turtle Power during Saturday-morning TV in 1989. With a follow-up movie, T-shirts, pajamas, lunch boxes and videos, Teenage Mutant Ninja Turtles sold themselves.

Splinter, the hero, accidentally turned from a man to a rat when a "mutagen" invaded his body. He lives with the Ninja Turtles—Michelangelo, Donatello, Leonardo and Raphael. Splinter is their teacher and friend. From the sewers of New York, they are the guardians of goodness. For now, dudes, the world is safe, thanks to Turtle Power. Cowabunga!

WALLS COME TUMBLING DOWN

The gates of the Berlin Wall swung open on November 9. It was a night that changed history. Many East Germans had only dreamed of freedom and democracy. Impossible as it seemed, they were now given freedom to leave. Thousands of East Berliners swarmed through the gate to West Berlin. There was cheering, clapping, dancing and weeping. Some came to West Berlin to stay. Many more came to sample the delights of freedom. They would then return to their homes. East and West Germans celebrated the tearing down of the wall that had divided them since the end of World War II. The world looked on.

Throughout Eastern Europe, people wanted changes in government. They wanted more freedom to rule themselves. The doors had been opened by Gorbachev's proposals for *glasnost* and *perestroika*. People looked forward to new freedoms and choices. The world was becoming a better place.

1989

45

The Teenage Mutant Ninja Turtles—heroes in a half shell

INDEX